Dare To Be Different

by

Terry L. Duperon
David M. Hall
John A. Dunn

"A dream is a vision that will have you
doing something different and better."

Acknowledgements

The authors acknowledge with grateful appreciation the
help and support of:

Kathy Conklin

Leslie Duperon

Chris Krieger

and others who encouraged this publication.

Table of Contents

I

Introduction

"It has occurred to me recently that I have never chosen anything. I was born with a role that had been prepared for me. I did everything I was asked to do because it never occurred to me to choose otherwise. And now at the end of life, I wonder what might have been."

Centauri Emperor Turhan, Babylon 5

People have pondered the question for hundreds of years, of what might have happened if we had pursued the dreams of our hearts. Today we proclaim, "What if . . . ?" and continue to ponder the question.

Each morning when we awaken does our every thought and action lead us closer to our heart's desire or does it lead us farther away from our dream? If we find that it leads us farther away from our dreams, we must ask the questions, "What can I do to get on course to be what I was created to be?" "What is important to me?" and "Do I have a calling?"

Are you working at a job that is not satisfying?

Are you in a business relationship that is not fulfilling?

Why are you staying in unfulfilling places?

Are you a prisoner of the current situation?

Who is holding you captive to these unfulfilling situations?

Does your work fulfill you?

What must be done to move on?

A recent study by the Conference Board notes that nearly half of U. S. workers are unhappy in their jobs. The survey showed as the baby boomers are replaced with younger workers, they are dissatisfied. Job dissatisfaction is a real issue in the workplace.

Could your thoughts, actions and training be keeping you in the mindset of unhappiness? Could fear of the unknown, beyond the walls of comfort, be keeping you from making a change?

Meet a young man seeking the freedom to become what he knows he was destined to be. He sought wisdom. This is the advice he received.

II

Letter from Son

Dear Dad:

I remember you once talking about "defining moments" in life. I've often wondered what that really means. I also wonder if I would know such a moment when it came or whether I would fail to recognize it until it had come and gone. As I evaluate my life — where I am and where I wish to go, I think I may be at such a defining moment.

I am looking at the things that drive me — my values. As you taught me, values control our behavior. I am grateful for the values that you and mom instilled in me. In addition to these, I have been blessed to have had a wonderful education all the way from kindergarten to my MBA. Because of this sterling preparation, I have been able to secure a great position with a Fortune 500 firm. I am told I have great career potential.

My bosses have nurtured me and mentored me. I have enjoyed several promotions and gained a wide array of experiences. The salary is superb. The people are personable and we share similar values. The potential for greater things in the future is good. I have already built a sizable portfolio that can sustain me in retirement.

But the fact is I feel unfulfilled in this job and in this career field. The question is why? You've always said, "People should be happy in their work. If not, they should find something else to do." As I assess this it makes me wonder why I am at this juncture of my life. Is this a defining

3

moment? I think I am at that fork in the road. It may be time for me to find something else to do.

For years I have harbored a dream—a dream of doing something else. I want to make a difference in the world and add to society in some way. As I look around everyday, I see so many opportunities. Surely some of them can be possibilities for me to pursue and make a difference. Are they worth consideration?

You always said to consider all options before making a decision. It seems to me that I have but two options. I can either stay at my present job and be unhappy for the rest of my career, or I can leave and chase my dream.

Remember the accountant you used to work with who was unhappy with his job? You challenged him to quit if he was so unhappy. He assured you he would as soon as his last kid completed college. He held on for the sake of his child. He suffered unhappiness to ensure that his child might have a chance for better opportunities. He held on in the hope that he was preparing his child to see greater possibilities. And finally, when the last kid completed his undergraduate degree, he quit. I do not have any such obligations holding me back. I am free to choose to stay or to move on now. The question remains, "What do I do?"

I know there is probably no easy answer. I have tried to recall all the advice and counsel you shared with me through the years. But I am still in a quandary. Help! This is why I am writing to you.

I probably should have asked face-to-face when we last met. Somehow I was not ready then. But I feel a new sense of urgency now. I would really appreciate your advice. I am struggling.

1. Is this one of those defining moments of life?

2. Is this normal?

3. How do you know or decide what to do?

4. What is the likelihood of success?

5. What have others done when going through this process?

6. How will I know when my dream has been fulfilled?

This is just the beginning of the many questions that invade my mind. Your help would be greatly appreciated.

Love,

Your son

III

What is Your Heart's Desire?
What Do You Love to Do?

Dear Son:

This letter may be a little longer than you might have imagined. What you are dealing with is not an uncomplicated dilemma. On second thought, I will try to answer you in a series of letters. Each will have a different focus. Each will add to your storehouse of knowledge. Each will move you closer to the action you should take for your future. Please recognize, I can only make you aware of options, opportunities and possibilities. The final decision is yours and yours alone.

Benjamin Mays said, "In order to withstand the troubles of this world one must have a sense of mission and a belief that God put him or her on this earth to do a specific thing. If it is not done the world is worse because it was not done." This suggests to me that God placed a dream on your heart when you were born. Your development through the years was preparation for the fulfillment of that dream.

That dream manifests itself in your desire to do something different. The dream gives us a mission to help mankind. That dream will be revealed to you at a given time. When it is, you will see opportunities and possibilities that will assist you in making your dream a reality.

What is a dream anyway? It may be described as unrest in your psyche that leads you to something that you are not now doing. A dream is that vision you have for the future.

7

A dream is a vision that will have you doing something different and better.

Let's look at where you have been. You began by having a structured life. When you think about it everything was by prescription. It was predetermined. The diagram illustrates where you have been and the process that you went through to get where you are.

Your schooling has given you a good foundation to solve problems and make decisions. In addition, it has helped you to see the need for continuous education. You were trained to follow a career ladder for a management and/or technical career. Through the years you have done well and developed your skills. You should be proud of your accomplishments.

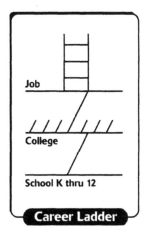

K – 12 education – college preparation/technical school

You have obtained the basics and you have specialized. This will serve you well now and in the future, whatever you decide to do. You even took your education to a higher level and learned about the management of different kinds of resources. Your life encompasses the diagram above. This education has prepared you with technical learning in a particular field that will serve you in good stead in the future, whatever you decide to do.

You have done well in your chosen field, but it could be that you are ready for something more.

Before we go any further, let us destroy a couple of well known myths:

Myth number 1: Only an idiot would leave a good job with a promising career in order to chase a dream.

If this were true, there would be many idiots in the world. Not only are such people not idiots, they are highly intelligent individuals who quit their jobs to chase their dreams.

Tom Watson left a good job at National Cash Register (NCR) Company, went home to New York and operated out of his parents' garage until he was able to get his dream working. His company developed Punched Card Accounting Machines and Computers and provided a variety of services to its customers. They also experimented with memory so that it could be enlarged and process faster. From a garage to one of the world's largest and most prosperous companies is not a bad journey. His company's new name - International Business Machines (IBM).

Remember H. Ross Perot? He ran for president of the United States back in 1992 and 1996. At one time he was the top salesman at IBM. He tried to convince IBM to adopt his idea. They wouldn't. Perot quit his job at IBM and started his own company called Electronic Data Systems (EDS). He was so successful that General Motors bought the company and depended on EDS to help solve their computer problems. Guess who became his chief competitor? It was IBM. I assure you Perot is worth more now than he would have been if he had stayed at IBM. Perot followed his dream and formed the largest facilities management firm in the nation.

Myth number 2: The only reason a person would leave a good job and career is to be assured of making more money.

Some wise old unidentified philosopher once said, "A true professional is one who concerns himself with salary as long as he is able to do what he is passionate about." This does not mean that passionate people should work for peanuts. They want and expect decent wages, but money is not the big concern.

In my hometown I know two men who were successful in the workforce but were willing to give it up to chase their dream — their passion. One was a bank executive, the other a partner in a sizable law firm. They were not the happiest doing what they were doing. They quit their jobs, went to divinity school, and qualified themselves to be ministers. Both started out at small churches. Both had wives who supported their dream by working until they were able to get a church that could give them a livable wage. These men followed their dream. Today they are both successful in their new career field. Theirs was a dream, a real calling — a passion.

Conversely, there is a former priest who gave up one calling for another. He gave up the priesthood to become a lawyer. He is now a partner in a medium-sized law firm with several other lawyers. He has a reputation for being a good lawyer.

I am willing to bet that he was also a good priest. But he saw a different dream and pursued it.

Myth number 3: People leave their jobs because they want to be their own boss. I am sure somewhere, at some time, people have left their jobs just because they wanted to be their own boss. These people probably left for the wrong reason.

People do leave their jobs to chase dreams. In the book *Mary K*, author Mary Kay Ash left hers because she believed she could do it better. She started out in her kitchen at the kitchen table and created a line of cosmetic products and a delivery system that is the envy of the cosmetics industry. She developed and perfected her idea. In the end she did do it better.

Myth number 4: People leave a job because they are unhappy.

Some people do reach a point where they can't stand to be in a particular environment. And it's a fact that most unhappy people look for another job. A person who has a dream, however, is not necessarily unhappy, but unfulfilled. If you are unhappy there is something you do not like. Unhappiness, although self imposed, is normally triggered by external influences. The term "unfulfilled" suggests that your inner satisfaction is not good. You do not feel that you are contributing your best to the improvement of the enterprise, society or yourself.

There are many more myths associated with people leaving their current job and chasing a dream. Most, if not all, are without merit. That is why they're called myths. Now that we have destroyed the more popular myths, you must ask yourself the most important question. "Why do I want to change jobs?" "Why am I dissatisfied?"

I am sure that somewhere in your school life you took at least one examination that gave you an indication of what you are suited for. There are also personality and temperament tests. All of these are designed to assist people in understanding who they are.

The real answer to these tests is deep down in your own soul. What *are* your interests? What are you passionate about? What motivates you? What causes you to take the initiative? What is in you? If the answer to these questions point in one direction, then that is who you are.

You do not have to conform and do what everyone else has done. You do need to do what makes you happy. Happiness comes from being true to yourself and following your dream. Look around you and see the opportunities and possibilities. Leave yourself open to suggestions and new ideas, and you will see these opportunities and possibilities. If one of them matches your dream, you have made a connection. Your passion will see you through.

Enough for now! I will write you another letter later and further discuss your dream.

Love,

Dad

Lessons learned:

1. Fulfillment in life will never occur running with the crowd. Fulfillment comes from breaking away and following you heart.

2. Just because you are prepared for a career does not mean your heart is in it.

3. What you love to do today may not be what you love to do tomorrow.

Quotes:

"Desire creates the power."
   Raymond Holliwell

"There are two tragedies in life. One is not to get your heart's dream. The other is to get it."
   George Bernard Shaw

"Do you know what the greatest test is? Do you still get excited about what you do when you get up in the morning?"
   David Halberstam

"If a man does not keep pace with his companions, perhaps it is because he hears a different drummer. Let him step to the music which he hears, however measured or far away."
   Henry David Thoreau

IV

Faith

Dear Son:

I remember that as a young child, whenever you received something new, your first impulse was to tear it apart. It was not done in a destructive way. You were always inquisitive. It was like you were asking, "How did they put this together?" After the toy was in a million pieces, you began the long tortuous road of putting it back together. Whenever you completed the process, there always was a part or two or three left over. This became a challenge to you and you could spend long periods of time struggling with where the part went and what purpose it served.

You were a curious kid. You wanted to know. This is an important attribute to have. You have kept that desire to understand the unknown all of your life. It goes a long way in making you a success. In addition to inquiry, you must have faith. "Faith is the substance of things hoped for, the evidence of things not seen!" (Hebrew 11:1)

Faith is a set of principles or beliefs that one lives by. They serve as a foundation for living. Faith is a belief system. That belief system should include:

1. **Belief in self:** We live in a world that bombards us with negativism. It is sometimes difficult to tune out the negativism and get on with our own hopes and dreams. You may not remember now, but as a child you were exposed to a story called "The Little Train

That Could." The essence of the story is that there are times in your life when the road will be rough or steep. Those are the times that you would normally want to give up, quit, go back to the beginning or even rethink the need for the journey. The little train had a mantra that it sang as it tried to climb the hill using all of its energy and might. That mantra was, "I think I can, I think I can, I think I can!"

That is what belief in self is all about — believing in oneself. If you believe in yourself, all that negative energy swirling around you will not even make a dent in your belief system. Believing in yourself gives you the courage to start something new — something that has not been done before. You will find that you will be fearful, scared, nervous and reluctant. With belief in self you can start before you have a complete game plan on how things will come out. You take a step on faith. You hope for it but you have no way of seeing how it will happen. You are like the swimmer who places his toe in the water to gauge the temperature. If the toe feels warm, he will probably dive in. If the toe feels cold then he will enter the water a little at a time until his body acclimates to the temperature. Usually he will put legs in first at the shallow end. He will walk toward the deeper water until his waist is reached. These are periods of pause to help the body acclimate. Then he proceeds a little deeper until the entire body is covered. Notice there was no thought of quitting, getting out, or even rethinking whether he will swim. The only thing here is the speed with which he will eventually acclimate to the water.

Faith gives you that ability. When you start, you must start believing that whatever you need will appear when it is needed.

2. **Belief in mankind:** Most people are pretty good. There are times when you will begin to doubt yourself and the choices you have made. It is at this time that someone or something comes along that causes you to renew your faith.

   I am reminded of the young man who was in trouble with the law. He appeared before the judge. The judge, after listening to the case, the facts and circumstances, told the young man he had two options: he could either go to jail or he could join the service. The young man opted for the service.

   He enlisted in the Navy but he was paranoid. He did not believe anyone had his best interest at heart. He just did not believe anyone cared. He somehow managed to survive basic training and skill training and was assigned to a ship. At some point late in his sixth month of sea duty, the bridge officer told him it was his duty to man the bridge. The officer disappeared. Suddenly the young man was alone with the responsibility of a ship of many tons valued at billions of dollars. He realized that if someone else had faith that he could do it, then he too should have that faith. If people know what you want, they will help you. If people see you struggling as the young man struggled, some will try to aid you also.

3. **Belief in leadership:** Everyone works for someone. Never forget that. Even if you are the top dog in your organization (president or CEO), you still work for

someone. We all ultimately work for the customer. Never forget that. If the customer is unhappy, everyone will eventually be unhappy. The customer causes the income. No income — no company; no company — no jobs; no jobs — no profit.

Ideally, the person you work for is your leader. You have had many bosses. If you are lucky, you have had one or two real leaders. In my entire working career I have had hundreds of bosses and supervisors, but I have had only five real leaders. These are the people for whom you will do anything. You will follow them wherever they go. You will go wherever they tell you. You will do their bidding. Why?

You follow them because there is a trusting relationship between you. They are trustworthy and you trust them. That trust is based on the fact that they respect you. They treat you as a partner when it involves making decisions that impact you. You never wonder what your status is in the organization. They are always candid with you. They may ask you to do something that, on the surface, sounds dumb, but because of the relationship and the trust, you do it anyway. If the reason does not become evident in the process, you know if you ask, you will get a full explanation. So, you "press on!" Always build relationships with people — all people.

4. **Belief in our peers:** I have always lived by the philosophy that I will trust everyone until they give me reason not to. It has been my experience that if you and a peer have the same goal(s), you will generally agree on the right thing to do to achieve those goals. When you do disagree it is normally a

disagreement over method, approach, or process. Goals are the key. We must have clear goals and they must be understood the same way by all—peers, bosses, and subordinates alike.

5. **Belief in our subordinates / associates:** Years ago people who worked for you were called subordinates. Nowadays in most companies these subordinates are referred to as associates. Subordination suggests that you do what you are told. Subordinates were expected to do what they were told, when they were told. In other words, the subordinate had no requirement to think, suggest or improve on the process.

That is not true today. The world of management in business is trying hard to change by being more inclusive and getting input from their subordinates. Since providing input requires effort on the part of the subordinate and this effort is considered in forming and amending the process, associates can become a part of the decision process. The associate then is expected to have a voice and raise that voice when things can be done better, or when things seem to be going awry.

Our faith tells us that the associate, armed with the same goals, will craft plans and events that will make the process more efficient.

I am reminded of a story of two men, Calvin and Fred, working in a plant and producing a finished product for their company. Calvin was reporting to work to replace Fred.

"How's it going, Fred?"

Fred responded dejectedly, "It's going. The only thing I've done is make several hours of scrap."

"Scrap!" exclaimed Calvin.

"Yep," said Fred, "The tolerances are off and I have been making parts most of the day that do not meet specification."

"Did you tell the supervisor?" asked Calvin.

"Yes, he agreed to call the repair folk and he instructed me to continue to make product until they arrived. Actually, I could fix it myself in about an hour if I could stop the assembly line."

Fred did not believe that management would support his doing something outside his normal duties. He was a subordinate. He was doing what he was told. He had his instructions memorized and he followed them exactly. He had no faith in the possibility that if he had stopped the process and fixed the machine he may have been appreciated for saving the process and insuring a quality product.

Faith can move mountains — only if we take the first step.

Love,

Dad

Lessons learned:

1. Faith is acting on what you believe.

2. Faith requires a relationship of trust.

3. Faith makes the impossible possible.

4. The biggest mistake in life is not acting on your faith.

5. Faith can move mountains.

Quotes:

"A strong positive mental attitude will create more miracles than any wonder drug."
Patricia Neal

"To convince them, you must yourself believe."
Sir Winston Churchill

"The difference between the impossible and the possible lies in a person's determination."
Tommy Lasorda

"Whatever God's dream about man may be, it seems certain it can't come true unless man cooperates."
Stella Terrill Mann

V

Opportunities and Possibilities

Dear Son:

Let's examine this concept of opportunities and possibilities. We all have opportunities. That does not mean every opportunity is a possibility – at that time. The idea is to be prepared for opportunities when they arise. When you are prepared, the opportunity becomes a possibility.

You have prepared yourself. Look at the path you followed in education. Since graduation, your experiences have been amazing. You are prepared for opportunities, and your education and experiences make these opportunities possible.

Be open to ideas, suggestions and opportunities from everyone, as you make the transition from where you are to where you want to be. The true possibilities will be impossible to miss.

I am reminded of the story of a man in a gathering and hunting society seeking to feed his family. The goal of his hunting expedition was to kill a deer. He prepared all of his equipment, honed his skills and set out into the woods. The family evening meal and life itself depended on the outcome of this hunting trip.

He wandered through the woods to his favorite spot. He heard the chirping of the squirrels as they ate nuts found near the trees. A rabbit ran across his path as he was positioning himself. He broke a limb off a bush filled with berries, so he could get a better view of the path where the deer usually traveled. A couple of wild turkeys walked across the feeding spot he had established for the deer. While awaiting the deer, he decided to get a drink of water from a nearby brook filled with trout. The man practiced all the skills he had learned from his father who was a master hunter, with no results. He returned home that night stepping on wild mushrooms with no food for the family.

Because he had a preconceived notion of what the outcome should be, he passed up some possibilities. He was blind to the possibilities that were in front of him. To take advantage of opportunities and possibilities, you must be like a soldier in survival training. You have no notion of what may be available to you so you look for opportunities and possibilities that you can take advantage of.

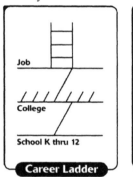

Note, the right side above is free of barriers and constraints. Your mind needs to be the same way when it comes to deciding how to approach your future. There is so much help out there that you will find the opportunities and possibilities endless.

Your education and experiences have prepared you for many things, but not for the entrepreneurial world. In this world, there are four "hats." Each hat represents the following different knowledge and talents:

Management Hat:

- Works through others – delegates.

- Delegates authority but keeps the responsibility.

- Responsibilities include but not limited to:

  o Planning
  o Organizing
  o Staffing
  o Coordinating
  o Motivating
  o Leading
  o Controlling

- Responsible for manifesting the entrepreneur's vision as a system that operates the business/organization.

Technician Hat:

- Has a practical understanding of the theoretical principles of that field.

- Expert in a particular art or brand of knowledge.

- Desires to perform the day-to-day duties.

- Knows how to do specialized technical work.

- Technicians "go to work," but feel no true responsibility for what they do.

- Not interested in the business aspects.

Leadership Hat:

- Selects, equips, trains and influences the followers who have diverse gifts, abilities and skills.

- Creates a focus for the followers.

- Crafts a vision for the future of the enterprise.

(Source = *A Complete Definition of Leadership* by Bruce E. Winston 2003)

Entrepreneur Hat:

- Undertakes risk.

- Organizes the venture, business or trade.

- Helpful unique character traits include the following:

  o Natural charismatic leader.
  o Passionate about what they do.
  o Has vision and goals.
  o Is focused.
  o Creative problem solver.
  o Knows when to be flexible.
  o Is on a mission.
  o Relies heavily on intuition.
  o Responds best to challenges.
  o Relies on relationships and personal credibility.
  o Can visualize and dream their plans.

The Responsible Entrepreneur: Craig Hall

It sounds like you are considering entering the entrepreneurial world. This requires leadership. Leadership is about building relationships so that people will trust you. In order to have that happen you must do things to make you trustworthy. Do what you say you will do. Keep your word. It is the only thing you can give away and still keep. Help those who are struggling. Have a positive attitude. Develop an abundance mentality. By doing these things you are modeling behavior that will serve you well with anyone. That is what leadership is all about.

Life is a canvas on which we can paint anything we desire. This blank canvas must have leadership. There is another hat that is equally important. That is the hat of the entrepreneur.

An entrepreneur who is a leader has a better chance of success than the person with the brightest and best idea but has no leadership. Nokia at one time took the lead in cellular telephones from Motorola by showing leadership. On the other hand, although late getting into the PC market, IBM rose to leadership in the field of personal computers. But then, Dell became the leader in the PC market. Did they have the best PC? Probably not. They became the leader by changing their distribution and manufacturing process.

Leadership and entrepreneurship are, at minimum, Siamese twins when it comes to starting your own business or inventing something new.

The entrepreneur is a change agent. The entrepreneur has an idea that will change the world, or some portion of it in a way that has not been done before. The entrepreneur initially faces negativism. People do not like to be changed. People, when they find their comfort zone, they like to stay in it as long as possible. Thomas Alva Edison tried over 1000 ways to make the incandescent light bulb work. Can't you imagine his friends and peers looking at him askance and concluding that he may have a small-to-medium-sized crack in his brain? To them it must have looked ridiculous to keep trying. But persistence paid off. He was successful.

Initially, many people resist using something new. Many people will not buy a car the first year it is introduced or give new and exciting software a try. They wait to see what defects are identified by the early buyers. Then they give the manufacturer a year or two to correct the defects and then they purchase defect-free cars or software. This is begrudging acceptance.

After others are found to enjoy new technology and greater efficiency, the reluctant then embraces the new technology with enthusiasm and uses it to the advantage of their enterprise.

These four steps are forever present when you decide to make change:

Step 1: Negativism

Step 2: Resistance

Step 3: Begrudging acceptance

Step 4: Acceptance

You have a responsibility as an entrepreneur. Whatever you propose and invest your time and money into must make conditions better. People will not make changes when there is no promise of improvement. Always, as you plan, plan for the new to be better.

Let leadership and entrepreneurship together be your compass. The enclosed chart on entrepreneur traits from *The Responsible Entrepreneurs: How to make money and make a difference* may be useful.

Love,

Dad

Entrepreneur traits:

"Entrepreneurs are individuals who understand the
responsibility of uncertainty.... They are decision-makers
who improvise solutions to problems which cannot be
solved by some routine method. They are adventurers
seeking the pursuit of fulfilling their passion and dreams,
daring to assume the rewards of success and the risk of
failure in birthing their own venture.

- Natural charismatic leader
- Passionate about what they do
- Have vision and goals
- Think out of the box
- Work hard and hopefully smart
- Are survivors
- Trying to prove themselves
- Are focused
- Are optimistic
- Are realistic when they need to be
- Creative problem solvers
- Are often insecure
- Never give up
- Know when to be flexible
- Are motivators
- Are on a mission
- Can "pull the trigger" on decisions
- Are angry, frustrated and hungry for control
- Are introspective
- Rely heavily on intuition
- Emotional and sensitive
- Use win-win approach
- Respond best to challenges
- Rely on relationships and personal credibility

- Don't accept failure; keep trying
- Can visualize and dream their plan
- Stress carriers who handle pressure well
- Are responsible"

Hall, Craig, *The Responsible Entrepreneur: How to make money and make a difference*, Careers Business Information, 2001.

Lessons learned:

1. Opportunities exist in abundance.

2. An entrepreneur has the ability to see the invisible (dream).

3. You must be who you are and do what comes naturally.

4. You must build relationships based on trust.

Quotes:

"The moment of enlightenment is when a person's dreams of possibilities become images of probabilities."
   Vic Braden

"Some opportunities are often the beginning of great enterprises."
   Demosthenes

"There is no security on this earth, there is only opportunity."
   Gen Douglas MacArthur

"If you can dream it, you can do it."
   Walt Disney

VI

Share your Dreams

Dear Son:

It was John Donne who said, "No man is an island, no man stands alone." Grab hold of that philosophy. You are not in this venture alone. What you must do is share your dreams. There are those who will help you accomplish your dreams if they know and understand them. Dreams allow you to see things you couldn't see before. There is power in dreaming.

Sometimes I feel we live in a negative world, so don't be surprised if not every person with whom you share your dream is a supporter or encourager. There seem to be more negative people than positive people. There seems to be an abundance of people who can tell you what is wrong with everything.

I had a recent discussion with your Uncle Hans on negative versus positive people. He related that he asks his clients to tell him three good things about their circumstances before they begin to tell him why he is being considered as their attorney. Invariably, they will tell him one positive thing and then launch into a sea of negativism. In his many years of practicing law and asking that question he has yet to find a client who has given him three good things. Only a few have made it to two positive comments.

However, there is power in partnering with the right individual to make your impossible dream a reality. It is a quick and easy way to overcome your lack of knowledge in a particular area of expertise. Partnering provides access to resources beyond your imagination. The benefits of effective partnering are examined in Steven C. Scott's book, *Mentored by a Millionaire*. Great success can be attributed to the partnering of the right individuals at the right time and in the right place. Great failures will have no partners or poor partnering as a foundation for the disaster.

Find and surround yourself with positive people. They believe in life and believe in enjoying life and making a difference. These are the people who will help you with your dream. You don't do it by yourself. Avoid negative people. They will find fault with your idea, your approach, and eventually with you, especially if you persist in spite of their negativity. The following is a typical scenario:

A young man expressed to his business professor a desire to start his own business. The professor's depressing response was, "You cannot do that. You are not ready. You don't have the experience, capital, nor business acumen. You should concentrate on your degree, which is why you are here."

The same young man shared his dream with one of his roommates. "Yeah, John, you would be a great business owner. I think you should quit school and go for it." After John departed the room, the roommate remarked, "Where did John get the crazy idea of going into business?"

Look deeper. Get to know the person through a relationship. The real person will surface. These people are equally determined. They contribute only what you already know, adding nothing to the equation. More sophisticated yes men will reword your thoughts and give them back to you. Have you experienced this type of person?

This does not mean you shouldn't seek people who disagree with you. Actually they are apt to be your best friend while you are chasing your dream. First, they bring a new perspective. Their view will be different from yours and it will cause you to ponder their thoughts. This is good. Being open-minded you are likely to find much help from the person who thinks differently. President John F. Kennedy did this when he established his cabinet. He found people who differed from him philosophically. These people were of great help to the president in his decision-making process. He knew and understood a view different from his own. If the truth were known, I am willing to bet that he used the ideas and suggestions of others over his own several times during his administration. Disagreeing is good. Being disagreeable is not good.

Paul was obviously downhearted as he delivered a pizza to a neighbor. The customer asked him why he was so sad. Paul explained that his heart's desire was to own a business. The customer/neighbor smiled and said, "Young man you can do anything that you believe that you can do. Let no one steal your dream! If I can be of assistance, let me know." Paul felt a new hope.

Seek support from people who can help you. Some may turn you down. Most will be pleased to help. Maybe they missed the opportunity to pursue their own dream. Maybe they are just giving people by nature. Whatever the reason, you will find many positive people who are willing to help you on your journey.

Sam shared the dream of owning a business with his parents. His father replied, "Go for it. I wish you the best. I will support you!" Mother chimed in, "You should finish college first and work for a while before you think about a business." In the hour-long debate that followed, John heard both benefits and hazards regarding business start-ups. The discussion gave him insight and direction.

There will come a time when you feel you are stuck. You will have no idea who to trust. Your back will be against the wall and you will feel frustrated. This is when you should begin sharing your problems with the positive people you shared your dream with. One or more of them will introduce you to someone else who can help you come to a resolution.

When a friend of mine was working on his PhD, he found himself having difficulty with statistics. He was at a loss. He did not know who to turn to. One day he ran into one of his positive people who asked about his progress. With great reluctance, he confessed he was having difficulty with statistics. He had read book after book with no real breakthrough.

His positive friend told him of a person who could help. "But I don't know him," the PhD candidate proclaimed. "You don't have to know him. He enjoys statistical work. Actually he enjoys teaching statistics as well as he enjoys working with statistics." Because my friend shared his dream, he received help that he could not have otherwise imagined.

So my advice to you is find an anchor. An anchor is a person who will have faith in you regardless of what happens. These are your real friends. They will encourage you when you goof up and they will encourage you when you are doing well. Just make sure your anchor is a person with the capacity of being brutally honest. You need honesty. You don't want to have to guess what he is trying to tell you. A true anchor's approach would sound like, "What you did was dumb. Let me tell you why." You get the message clearly. There is no doubt. When this happens it is time to listen hard.

Over the years, Pete's pastor had taken a personal interest in his life. During Pete's periods of trials and conflict the pastor offered sound spiritual advice. Pete approached the pastor and shared his dream. He closed his dream discussion with, "Pastor, I depend on you to give me a straight answer. What do you think of my dream?"

"Pete, my son, I find nothing wrong with your dream. I would suggest, though, that you finish college while you continue to refine and pursue your dream. The additional education will lighten the load and reduce potential challenges along the way."

Dreams are but wishes. When we take that first step, that step in the dark, we are in the process of making the dream a reality. Dreams come true because someone sets a goal and takes action. Have you noticed that the first two letters of the word G O A L spell "GO"?

But whatever you do, please do not confuse a dream with a goal. A goal is when you have an idea of how to accomplish a specific task.

A dream is something beyond the experience and training you have. A dream is much more vague. When you decide to follow your dream you will find yourself stepping into uncharted waters. When you first have your dream, you will have no inkling of how you will accomplish it. You start by taking one step at a time. One of those steps is sharing your dream. Others can give you counsel and advice as you navigate the waters of the unknown.

In each instance the first step is GO. You must go and do something. In a goal you know just what to do, or you have a reasonable idea and lots of options – just in case. With a dream, you GO, but you start without prescription.

Go and share your dream with the right people and let them help you through the tough spots and you will be successful.

Enclosed is a thought from Bruce Wilkinson's book, *The Dream Giver.*

Love,

Dad

"DARE TO SHARE YOUR DREAMS:

The danger in sharing your dreams is often overlooked and people will kill it during the birth process. A dream is a new born baby, fragile, innocent and must be protected and nurtured until it can stand on its own. You can share your dream with the But Family or the Can Family. The But Family will make the following types of comments:

- But you don't have the background for that
- But what if . . . . .
- But are you really sure about that
- But you don't have the money
- But you know others have failed
- But you shouldn't leave your job
- But nobody knows you
- But you can't compete with the big boys
- But they will not let you do that

They will write excuses all over your dream script and fill the air with negative clouds filled with the rain of failure. Life is a blank canvas that we can paint a picture of what we would like it to be. Be careful to stay away from those whose mission in life is to scribble negative marks on your canvas. They are dream predators seeking to kill your unborn masterpiece.

Look for the Can Family who will give you encouragement, support and connections to turn your empty canvas into a masterpiece. They don't know the Buts nor do they care to meet them. The Can Family knows only can do. As you travel through life watch for the But Family."

Andrew Shims, www.PositiveMoneyIdeas.com, offers the following tips to keep the Buts from raining on your parade:

- "Reality check: know yourself — know what you are good at and what you're not good at. Know what drives you and what you are passionate about.

- Do your homework. Find out everything you can about your dream before you share it.

- Don't hang out with turkeys because they don't have a vision to fly. They will have you served up as Thanksgiving dinner. Your dreams will be smoked, baked and fried.

- Fly with eagles because they know what it takes to fly high above the crowd.

- Make your dreams real by writing down every dream or idea you have. This makes you accountable to vocalize and visualize your dream.

- Patience and persistence: If it is worth having, then it is worth struggling for. Attack the problem as you would eat an elephant. Take one bite at a time."

Family and friends can be supportive of your dream or be the primary roadblocks to your leaving the familiar to journey into the unknown. Bruce Wilkinson in his book *The Dream Giver* identifies two close relatives and a friend who attempt to block the dream of **Mr. Ordinary**:

"You mustn't go. I was so alarmed when I heard you were leaving Familiar. I know you told us that you were, but I never thought you would. Honestly, what are you thinking? It is not safe. You could get hurt. You could even die." **Ordinary Mother**

"Do you realize that you are going completely against every tradition in this family? Why should you become a Somebody when the rest of us have always been happy being Nobodies?" **Ordinary Uncle**

"I was worried before, Ordinary, but the more I thought about it, the more convinced I am that you can't succeed at this. I can't stand by and watch you go down in defeat." **Ordinary Best Friend**

There is a degree of comfort for relatives and friends in keeping you in comfortable surroundings. It keeps pressure off them to respond to your dreams. They are afraid of what will be lost if you move on. The traditional economic system needs a pool of workers who accept the ordinary and continue doing the unfulfilling work.

The journey will be filled with obstacles, challenges, roadblocks and giants, but you must be willing to confront them all. Gil Eagles comments, "If you want to be successful, you will be uncomfortable."

People are taught to stay in their comfort zones and never step into the unknown until they have the answers. Life is a journey not a trip. A trip can be planned with road maps, hotels, meals and significant landmarks. A journey is a venture into unknown places with unknown outcomes. The success of a journey is tied to the ability of the traveler to respond to the challenges and obstacles encountered. Don't let your family and friends convince you to abort your dreams.

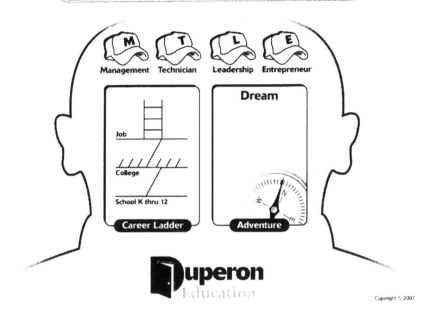

The American Dream

Management   **Technician**   **Leadership**   **Entrepreneur**

Dream

Job

College

School K thru 12

Career Ladder

Adventure

)uperon
Education

Sharing your dream helps you incorporate the other side. You have help in adding the entrepreneurial to the traditional. When you start that move you will be open to new and different possibilities and challenging opportunities. You need only your own compass to guide you. That guidance will come from your heart's desire.

Lessons learned:

1. Sharing your dreams will be necessary, but be prepared for dream killers.

2. Seek a variety of views.

3. Be careful how you handle responses from the negative sector.

4. Establish a relationship with a solid rock counselor or advisor.

5. Cultivate a cheering section. Go to them when you experience negativity.

Quotes:

"Do you dream big? You are limited by your dreams!"
    Tiger Woods

"No person has the right to rain on your dreams."
    Marian Wright Edelman

"Dare to err and to dream."
    Johann Friedrich von Schiller

"We need men who can dream of things that never were."
    John F. Kennedy

"The things that one must want to do are the things that are probably most worth doing."
    Winifred Holtty

VII

Strengths and Weaknesses

Dear Son:

This is not a discussion about your skills, training or
experience. This is about those God-given talents that seem
to be naturally easy for you. Things that we excel at, enjoy
and have a passion for, that seem to be built-in at birth.
These things are a part of our internal makeup. We were
created for a specific purpose, so our talents complement our
partners (marriage, business, religion, etc.) in life. Friends
and relatives will tell you about their passions and pursuits.
They seldom, if ever, tell you about their weaknesses.

At almost every job interview there is the inevitable
question, "What are your weaknesses?" Weaknesses are
looked upon as something negative. Weaknesses are looked
upon as something to be avoided. Weaknesses are looked
upon as things that we should never reveal. Weaknesses are
looked upon as something to repair or shore up in the back
room so no one is aware.

To put things in perspective, why should someone care
about your weaknesses? They bring nothing to the solution
of a problem or increasing the productivity in an
organization. We cannot be all things to all people. Those
who try are either overworked and end up with health
problems, or they do many things in a mediocre fashion.
Their true strengths never have the chance to surface.
Weaknesses can be our friend. If we are honest with
ourselves, we acknowledge our shortcomings. When we do,

we acknowledge to ourselves that we need help in that area. When we are honest enough to admit that we need help, the amazing thing is that most people help us. If we are able to get the help we need, why do we need to be an expert in the area where we are weak?

Too often people try to be too much to too many. "I don't know," and "Let me ask John," seem to be words of failure to many people. Saying, "I don't know" does not mean we don't care. It means we have an opportunity to learn. The phrase should be followed by, "I will find out." Likewise, "Let me ask John," should be followed by, "that is his area," or similar words. You are saying that it is not your area of strength.

We can't be an expert in everything. We can't know everything. This is why people work in teams in today's business world. The team concept suggests that you need teammates with different strengths. In this way everyone complements the other person. All skills needed for a particular task are available from some member of the team. In this way all skills needed to make the team successful are available to the entire team. This also gives each team member an opportunity to learn from the other team members. Consider this when you are sharing your dreams.

Try the exercise below and see if you are among the many who avoid acknowledging your own weaknesses, even to yourself.

1. Name five weaknesses.

2. Prioritize these weaknesses. (List in order of gravity.)

3. How can you overcome that number one weakness?

If you had difficulty naming five weaknesses, you are normal, because we tend to ignore them. Maybe that's a good thing. Maybe we should concentrate on our strengths. How do we overcome the weaknesses? We form alliances. We join teams. We share our dreams. We learn to accept help with humility.

WHO CARES ABOUT LISTING WEAKNESSES ANYWAY?

They don't help us get anything done.

THERE IS NO POWER IN WEAKNESSES.

A good leader will hire people with strengths in areas where the leader is weak. In this way the leader's strengths are complemented by the people hired. Most leaders feel that because of their position they are not supposed to have weaknesses. If they acknowledge their weaknesses to themselves, they make it a point to hide them from their people. It takes a real leader to admit weaknesses.

One of the advantages of acknowledging your weaknesses is that people learn that you are human. People already know that you cannot be all things to all people. People know that there are certain things that you do not do well. Why try to fool the people who work for and with you? When you as the leader fail to acknowledge your own weaknesses, you are considered a phony by your people. People know what their leader is good at. Likewise, they know the areas where the leader is weak.

Everyone has strengths. These strengths are used to add value to the organization. These strengths:

Help elevate the team. When people on the team carry their weight, the value of the team increases. People can work in harmony when they bring their expertise to focus on the team goal(s).

Fill a void. No one person can be an expert in everything. When one person tries to do the work of everyone on the team he will not be top performer in every aspect of all the tasks involved. Therein lies the need for a team. Team members are recruited to take care of the shortcomings of others.

Cause people to respect you. We all desire respect. Respect must be earned. We earn respect in many ways. One way is to contribute the expertise we have to the organization. In this way we are making the organization better.

Build our self-esteem. People feel good about themselves when they are equal contributors and partners in making something happen. High self-esteem improves attitude. People with high self-esteem do not hesitate to help others.

People with high self-esteem are the ones who act on their dreams without hesitation. One of the strengths of the entrepreneur is the ability to act without knowing what will happen. It is an act of faith. Sometimes we develop our strengths by taking an act of faith, by trying something.

I want to leave you with this final thought. Entrepreneurs need to be strong in their belief. They must have faith that their dreams can become reality.

Love,

Dad

Lessons learned:

1. It is important to recognize weaknesses.

2. Do not spend too much time on weaknesses.

3. Focus on building a team where every talent or requirement is covered.

4. Purchase the expertise if you cannot develop it.

5. It is impossible to be an expert in everything.

Quotes:

"A true friend knows your weaknesses but shows you your strengths; feels your fears but fortifies your facts, sees your anxieties but frees your spirit, recognizes your disabilities but emphasizes your possibilities."
William Arthur Ward

"My weaknesses . . .I wish I could come up with something. I probably would have the same pause if you ask me what my strengths are. Maybe they are the same thing."
Al Pacino

"I am a member of a team, and I rely on the team. I defer to it and sacrifice for it because the team, not the individual, is the ultimate champion."
Mia Hamm

VIII

Stepping Over the Edge

Dear Son:

The story is told that baby eagles are prone to enjoy the comfort of the nest. In order for them to test their wings, the mother has to push the baby eagles out. It would appear that the baby would not step over the edge without help from mother. Once the baby eagle is pushed out of the nest, the mother is flying along with the baby to help the little one in its first attempt to fly. Ahhhhhh, such comfort!

Stepping over the edge is like being in the dark. When you first enter a dark theatre, you can't see anything, but after a little while your eyes adjust and you can see shadows, movement and images. The images are not clear. They are fuzzy. They do let you see movement.

Before you enter the dark or step over the edge, you are in the realm of comfort. It is the realm you know best. It is the realm you understand. People dislike leaving comfort. When they decide to leave comfort, they know that there is greater reward in the new way of doing things. It was Nicolo Machiavelli, in 1513, who said:

> "It must be remembered that there is nothing more difficult to plan, more doubtful of success, nor more dangerous to manage, than the creation of a new system. For the initiator has the enmity of all who would profit by preservation of the old institution

and merely lukewarm defenders in those who would gain by the new one."

There is no comfort in doing things differently. It has its agony and anguish, but it is the rewards that we seek.

There are many ways in which we may end up over the edge.

One of those ways is through encouragement. Remember when you first tried to swim? You had watched others swim alone. You had some instructions from me. Yet, there was anxiety associated with being left in the water alone. It was interesting to watch you stroke out on your own for the first time. Even you admitted it was easier than you thought it would be.

You have seen other entrepreneurs quit their ordinary jobs and get started. You can do the same thing. They took that step in the dark with the knowledge that they did not know how things would turn out, but they kept going. As children we all tried to walk. What did we do? Each time we fell, we smiled, got up and tried again. We were optimistic. We were trying something new. We didn't even know if we were supposed to walk. We were stepping out in the dark.

I don't know why we grow up and lose that spirit and the ability to try things without knowing how they will turn out. Think about developers and designers of anything and you will discover that when they started, not only were they in the dark, their friends and neighbors probably thought they were a bit batty for trying to do something that had never been done. All new discoveries are made by people willing to step in the dark and focus on their dream.

Another motivator is dissatisfaction. I remember the first new car I ever purchased. The salesman asked me early in the discussion about the vehicle I was trying to replace. From then on he kept making comparisons between my old car and any number of options he could give me in a new car. His purpose was to increase my dissatisfaction with my present vehicle and encourage me to buy a new one from him.

It is human nature to evaluate our circumstances. You have indicated dissatisfaction with your present circumstances. When that level of dissatisfaction is high enough, you will be ready to take your own step in the dark. You will look upon it as an opportunity for something better than you have now. People change jobs because they are dissatisfied. People divorce because they are dissatisfied. They don't leave jobs or marriages the first time something goes wrong, but over time, as things continue to go wrong, they become dissatisfied enough to seek change. Change is stepping into the dark. You already know what you have. You have become dissatisfied with it. What you don't know is how things will be when you leave the job or the spouse. You are stepping in the dark.

Another motivating factor is that some people just have a desire for a better life, or maybe to make life better for someone else. They see opportunities and options that could leave them in better circumstances. It's all about what could be better. Great discoveries, such as penicillin, prednisone, and vitamins, just to name a few, are all created by people who wanted to make life better. The teams of people supporting the astronauts were people who created and discovered things to make living easier while in space. The rest of the world has enjoyed some of these discoveries and creations.

Every now and then people will get pushed into something unplanned. Sometimes they are pushed out of something they were comfortable with. If there were no pushing, children might stay at home forever. Why leave? The bed will hold two. The driveway will hold an additional car. There is food available and it is comfortable.

Parents have different ways of pushing the kids out. Sending them off to college and converting their room to a sewing room or a spa is one approach. Parents prepare kids psychologically for their departure. They talk about others who have left home and mention how well they are doing. They engage you in discussions about making it on your own. They teach you how to sew, cook and do minor repairs. It is all a part of the system designed to push you out at a certain age and time.

People will push themselves about as hard as they wish to be pushed. But, to get over the edge, we must push ourselves as hard as we know how toward the end we wish to achieve. Pushing others is easy. Pushing yourself is more difficult. There are a few things that help us self-push.

First, we must have the goal or objective in mind. Second, we must be flexible. The journey can take twists and turns that are unplanned but may lead to something even better. Third, we have to stay focused. I remember watching a golf match in which Tiger Woods was about to putt. Someone threw a piece of fruit across his path. He was so focused he never even flinched. He was able to completely ignore the fruit and focus on his ball. Incidentally, he made the putt.

Lastly, keep control of yourself. Establish your own timetables and review points.

The push/pull concept was developed in the manufacturing industry to control inventory. Push indicated storing and inventorying raw materials in order to have them when they were needed. The pull concept required the operations manager to determine what was required when and arrange to have that inventory delivered at the right time.

When you visit an automobile showroom a salesman will approach you. His goal in life is to pull you toward his idea of the car for you. His questions will center on money available to spend, lifestyle concerns, driving habits, and even employment. The salesman is now ready for the pitch and close. Many know how to pitch. Few know how to close. Closing is confidently asking for the sale or confirming the sale. It is a part of being pulled. You have just stepped over the edge when you sign on the dotted line.

Most people never step over the edge because they are busy weighing the consequences. I read an article once that described people as choosers. All people do is choose to do or not to do. We are no different as we approach fulfilling our dream. We must choose. What seems like over the edge will soon be your next comfort level, but we have to take the first step without knowing the consequences.

"Wait a minute," you say, but I say, "why wait?" We do this all the time. When we step out into the street we do not know the consequences. There is risk in everything. Most of what we do, we do not know the consequences. Franklin Delano Roosevelt said, "The only thing we have to fear is fear itself." So, get over fearing the consequences and step out. Someone described fear as, "False Evidence Appearing Real." No more false evidence in our lives! Step out!

Success or failure is directly related to our willingness to continue stepping over the edge and living out of our comfort zone. If you are comfortable, it is time to step over the edge again. Remember, you would still be crawling today if you hadn't taken that first step. Step over the edge.

I'm throwing in a little chart for your review. I lifted it from someone. I forget where.

Love,

Dad

STEPPING INTO THE UNKNOWN

Known (Natural realm)	Unknown (Spiritual realm)
Known **(Natural realm)**	**Unknown** **(Spiritual realm)**
Has been done	Never been done before
Pattern available	No map
Steps have been identified	No blueprint
Comfortable	Uncomfortable
Can be seen	Can only be imagined
Assistance available	No help available
Education and training	No education or training
Resources available	No resources available
Faith not needed	Faith required

Lessons learned:

1. We must move out of our comfort zone.

2. The darkness will become light when we work into it.

3. The journey will be a constant series of steps over the edge.

4. When we become comfortable, it is time to move.

5. We must overcome the fear of the unknown.

Quotes:

"Entrepreneurship is a journey of a thousand miles and it must be taken one step at a time."
     David M. Hall

"We stand today on the edge of a new frontier . . . .; a frontier of unknown opportunities and perils – a frontier of unfulfilled hopes and threats."
     John F. Kennedy

"A fear of the unknown keeps a lot of people from leaving a bad situation."
     Kathie Lee Gifford

"A dream is a creative vision for your life in the future. You must break out of your comfort zone and become comfortable with the unfamiliar and the unknown."
Dennis Waitley

IX

What Stops You?

Dear Son:

You are probably tired of me rambling so this one letter will be short. The question is, "What stops you from pursuing your dream?"

Let's make a list and consider some thoughts:

Time: I don't have the time to pursue my dream.

Money: It takes too much money – more than I have.

Expertise: I don't have the education for this.

Equipment: Where would I get the tools?

Fear: I am afraid of the unknown world.

Not sure: I have never tried anything like this.

What people think: What if I fail?

Age: No one has ever done this at my age.

The list could go on and on.

Actually these are excuses. Norman Vincent Peale wrote that he had a problem standing between him and his success. The problem was himself. Every reason you can think of can be overcome by one and only one. That person is you. If you succumb to any excuse at all, you will never reach your dream. Only you can get in your way. Like Peale, learn and press on!

Love,

Dad

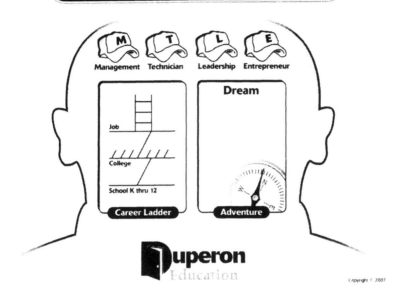

The American Dream

Management Technician Leadership Entrepreneur

Dream

Job

College

School K thru 12

Career Ladder

Adventure

Duperon
Education

There is the story of the young boy who approached his grandfather with a dilemma.

"Grandpa," he said, "there seems to be a struggle within me. It is like two wolves fighting. One is the good wolf. He is kind and considerate. The other is the bad wolf. He is evil and prone to doing wrong. Which one do you think will win?"

Grandpa replied, "The one you feed."

We all struggle between the tradition and the opportunities and possibilities that we see. Which one will you feed?

Lessons learned:

1. Fear is False Evidence Appearing Real!

2. "The only thing we have to fear is fear itself."
   Franklin Delano Roosevelt

3. You can overcome any excuse if you keep your eye on your dream.

4. Only you stand in the way of you!

5. The only one who stops you is YOU.

Quotes:

"We must constantly build dikes of courage to hold back the flood of fear."
   Martin Luther King

"Courage is not the absence of fear, but rather the judgment that something else is more important than fear."
   Ambrose Redmon

"To live a creative life, we must lose our fear of being wrong."
   Joseph Chilton Pearce

"Fear defeats more people than any other thing in the world."
   Ralph Waldo Emerson

X

Power

Dear Son:

Power is one of those words that is hard to define. It is like love. Everybody knows about it, nobody can tell you what it is. We all have power. Power comes from several sources. Two significant sources are the power that comes from some authority and the power that comes from the people. Power assists us in getting things done. We need power.

The third edition of *Webster's New World Dictionary* defines power many ways. There are fourteen definitions in all. A look at half of those will give you a clue as to where you should be along the power grid and how to use power in a way that it works for you instead of against you. Here are the definitions:

1. *Ability to do, act, or produce.* This indicates power is an action word. As a result of power, things get done by the person with the power. The question is, does the person with the power actually do the work or do they use their power to get others to do the work?

2. *A specific ability or faculty.* There is power in knowledge. People with knowledge power are consulted for advice and counsel. Could we say consultants have power? I remember working for a man named Max. Max's handwriting was so bad even he could not read it twenty-four hours

later. We depended on his secretary to translate his notes. She had power. Actually, she could make or break us.

3. *Great ability to do, act or affect strongly; vigor, force, strength.* In addition to performing, you have impact on others if you have power. That impact can take many forms. Modeling is one powerful form of power. If the boss comes to work in jeans each day we will tend to dress likewise. Should the boss choose to dress in suit and tie on a regular basis, we will tend dress in suit and tie. On the other hand, we could also exert our power by coercion. We can threaten another person with penalties or discipline if certain things are not done. Then again, we could use reward power.

4. *The ability to control others, authority, sway, influences.* People who hold office have authority over those in the organization for which they are responsible. The President of the United States has the authority over the armed services of the country. He gives the orders to the generals. Charles Manson, in his informal organization, gave orders to his followers to murder people and they implemented his command. There is power in leadership. This is the essence of power, convincing others to do what you want as if it were their own idea.

5. *Force or energy that is at or can be put to work.* Electric or water power come to mind. It could also include the autocratic manager. The water harnessed by the Hoover Dam generates millions of kilowatts of electricity. The forces of the wind

can power a windmill capable of generating electricity. Likewise, a person's energy not only can get more done, it can inspire others to exercise similar energy.

6. *The rate at which work is done.* There is power associated with speed and efficiency. A 1000 horsepower turbocharged engine is capable of propelling a 3000 pound car to speeds of 250 miles per hour in 60 seconds. A jet airplane engine demonstrates the same principle of speed and efficiency.

7. *A person or thing having great influence, force or authority.* We influence by our actions as well as by what we say. People respond better to authority when words and actions send the same message. Talk the talk and walk the walk. General Colin Powell had great influence over the foot soldiers during his reign in the military. He was a soldier's general. Because of his background, he had learned how to build relationships. He continued to build relationships with his soldiers and peers throughout his life.

These are but a few examples of power from a few different perspectives. As you can see, power can come from subordinates, peers or from some authority. There is power in your doing. There is power in the inference others take from your actions. Regardless of the source, we must learn how to effectively use power to influence others and get the job done.

Love,
Dad

Lessons learned:

1. Power is an active word.

2. Getting things done requires a source of power.

3. The ability to use power oftentimes determines the results.

4. Power can manifest itself in many ways.

5. Almost everyone has some power.

6. Too often many do not use the power they have.

Quotes:

"You're the writer, director and producer of your dreams."
Advertisement for Lincoln Motor Car

"Nearly all men can stand adversity, but if you want to test a man's character, give him power."
Abraham Lincoln

"Power is the faculty or capacity to act, the strength and potency to accomplish something; it is the vital energy to make choices and decisions. It also includes the capacity to overcome deeply embedded habits and to cultivate higher, more efficient ones."
George Bernard Shaw

XI

Afterword

Dear Dad:

Thanks for your letters. Your advice is helping me have a broader perspective and has given me hope. Some of the things I have learned from you are:

- Listen to my inner voice.
- Follow my dreams.
- Only I can take the first step. Step out on faith.
- Share my dreams during the journey.
- I don't have to know everything.

I know now that I need to get started.

Thanks for being there. I am lucky to have you.

Love,

Your son

XII

Dream Execution

November

Dear Dad:

Attached you will find a postcard that is being mailed to a selected mailing list soon. As you can see, as a result of your advice and wisdom, I have taken the leap.

I know you have been wondering what I've been doing. Now you know. It has been a long journey. Many people have helped me along the way. Some went so far as to find others with the expertise I needed to get started. It is truly amazing how things worked.

Thanks again for your help.

Love

Your son

Save the Date
Monday, January 1, 200_

A new date and a new beginning

The Grand Opening of

DHD Financial Services Corporation
Consulting, Training, Products and Service

Please join us for a reception at 5 PM
2600 Everywhere Street
Bring a guest and an appetite.

Regrets only at 989-555-1234

Reading List

Required Reading:

Gerber, Michael E.	*The E-Myth*
Littaur, Florence	*Personality Plus-How to Understand Others by Understanding Yourself*
Wilkinson, Bruce	*The Dream Giver*

Recommended Reading:

Hagberg, Janet O.	*Real Power*
Hall, Craig	*The Responsible Entrepreneur*
Hall, David M.	*The A, B, C's of Leadership*
Helmstetter, Shad	*What To Say When You Talk To Yourself*
Hill, Napoleon	*The Master Key to Riches*
Jackson, John	*Pastors and Entrepreneurs: Answer the Call*
Kiyosaki, Robert	*Rich Dad, Poor Dad*
Maxwell, John	*Be a People Person*

Megoinis, Alan Loy	*Bringing Out The Best in People*
Price, Fredrick	*How Faith Works*
Schwartz, David	*The Magic of Thinking Big*

Bibliography

Ashe, M. K. *Mary K: The Story of America's Most Dynamic Businesswoman.* New York: HarperCollins Publishers. Inc., 1994.

Bateman, T.; and S. Snell. *Management: Leading and Collaborating in a Competitive world.* 7th ed. New York: McGraw-Hill, 2007.

Benton, W, Publisher, Machiavelli, Nicolo, *The Prince,* Chicago: Encyclopedia Britannica, Inc., 1952.

Donne, John, *Meditations XVII*

Gerber, M. *E-Myth Mastery: The Seven Essential Disciplines for Building a World Class Company.* New York: Harper Business, 2003.

Hall, C. *The Responsible Entrepreneur: How to Make Money and Make a Difference.* Careers Business Information, 2001.

Holy Bible: Hebrews 11:1. Cleveland: World Publishing Co.

Jackson, J. *PastorPreneur: Pastors and Entrepreneurs Answer the Call.* Friend, TX: Baxter Press, 2003.

Maxwell, John. *The Difference Maker: Making Your Attitude Your Greatest Asset.* Nashville: Thomas Nelson, Inc., 2006.

Peabody, Bo. *Lucky or Smart: Secrets to an Entrepreneurial Life.* New York: Random House Publishing Group, 2005.

Scott, Steven C. *Mentored by a Millionaire.* Hoboken, NJ: John Wiley and Sons, 2004.

Roosevelt, Eleanor. *This Is My Story*. New York: Harper, 1937.

The Mescon Group, Inc. *Values: A Foundation for Success*. Cincinnati: Thompson Executive Press, 1995.

Webster's New World Dictionary, 3rd ed. New York: Prentice Hall, 1988.

Wilkinson, B; Kopp, D. and Kopp, H. *The Dream Giver*. Sisters, OR: Multnomah Publishing, Inc., 2003

Winston, B. E, and K. Patterson. *An Integrative Definition of Leadership*. Virginia Beach, VA: International Journal of Leadership, 2006.

Young Steve. *Great Failures of the Extremely Successful: Mistake, Adversity, Failure and Stepping Stones to Success*. Los Angeles: Tallfellow Press, Inc., 2002.

Web sites:

The Conference Board: http://www.conference-board.org/utilities

Shims, Andrew, www.PositiveMoneyIdeas.com

Made in the USA
Lexington, KY
02 December 2012